a visit to the AIRPORT

Ⓟ CHILDRENS PRESS ®

CHICAGO

by Sandra Ziegler

With special thanks to the staff at GENERAL MITCHELL INTERNATIONAL AIRPORT, Milwaukee, Wisconsin, where many of the scenes in this book were photographed.

Thank-you also to the children from TEACHING CENTERS, Milwaukee, Wisconsin, who worked with us so patiently.

Appreciation is also extended to UNITED AIRLINES and AMERICAN AIRLINES for making available existing photography.

The photographs in this book are intended to be representative of what children would see and do on a visit to a metropolitan airport and are not an exact reflection of any specific tour.

PHOTO CREDITS

PILOT PRODUCTIONS, INC.
   Dave Holmes, photographer
   Jay Kelly, lighting assistant
   Dean Garrison, director

Photos on pages 8, 12, 14, 15, 26, 31
   courtesy of AMERICAN AIRLINES.

Photos on pages 1, 7, 17, 18, 21, 22, 23, 24, 25,
   27, courtesy of UNITED AIRLINES.

Photo on page 24 by Susan Kazlaw-Ryan.

Library of Congress Cataloging in Publication Data

Ziegler, Sandra 1938-
   A visit to the airport.

   (Field trip books)
   Summary: A class visits an airport and observes
a wide variety of activities there.
   1. Airports—Juvenile literature.   [1. Airports]
I. Title. II. Series.
TL725.Z54 1988   387.7'36   87-35470
ISBN 0-516-01488-9

   2 3 4 5 6 7 8 9 10 11 12 R 96 95 94 93 92 91 90 89

a visit to the AIRPORT

Created by The Child's World

Kings Highway

7351

"Here comes a guide now," says Karen.
"Maybe he's coming to meet us."

Mrs. Dolan's class is excited. They have
come to visit the airport. They are eager to
see what it's like.

"Hello, everyone," says the guide. "My name is Mike Casper. I will go with you on your visit today." He smiles. The children smile back.

"Let's ride upstairs on the escalator," he says. And he leads the way.

The children follow Mr. Casper upstairs.
"This is where many passengers who
come to the airport first enter the terminal," he says. "But let's start our visit by
going outside to watch the people who
are arriving."

Outside the terminal, cars, taxis, and buses come and go. Horns beep. People scurry about. A business traveler pays for her ride to the airport. Nearby, a skycap waits. Helping with suitcases is his job. He will put a tag on each bag to show where the suitcase is going.

Back inside again, Mr. Casper says, "Everyone needs a ticket to ride on an airplane. Passengers can buy tickets at the airline ticket counters."

"How will that lady know where to go to get on her airplane?" asks Tracy. "The airport is so big."

Mr. Casper shows the children a picture map. "Passengers board their airplanes at gates," he says. "Every flight has a gate number. One way to find where you are and where you want to go is by looking at the airport map.

"We want to go to gate E-65," he adds.

To go to a gate, everyone must pass
through a security check. Tracy goes first.
Then Mr. Casper tells Jill, Karen, and Peter
that a buzzer will sound if something goes
through that shouldn't. It's quiet when they
go through.

David, Carlos, Brenda, and John stop to watch the small bags and purses coming through another security machine. Mr. Casper explains that the machine takes X-rays of the bags. The X-rays show what's inside each one.

Walking along, the children pass several boarding areas. People are sitting or standing, waiting for their planes. Some read. Others visit. A few just people-watch.

At one waiting room, the children go to a window to watch the busy workers outside.

When they arrive at gate E-65, the plane is not there yet. Mr. Casper shows the children the special walkway the passengers will use to get off the airplane when it arrives.

He also shows them lots of other planes,
waiting at other gates.

"Look," says Mrs. Dolan. "A plane has just landed." The children watch as the man on the ground directs the pilot up to gate E-65.

"That's the plane we are going to visit," says Mr. Casper.

The children wait for the passengers to
get off. Then they follow Mr. Casper onto
the plane. First they try out the seats. Then
Mr. Casper tells them about oxygen masks.
He says that most passengers never need
to use one. Masks are just there for emer-
gencies.

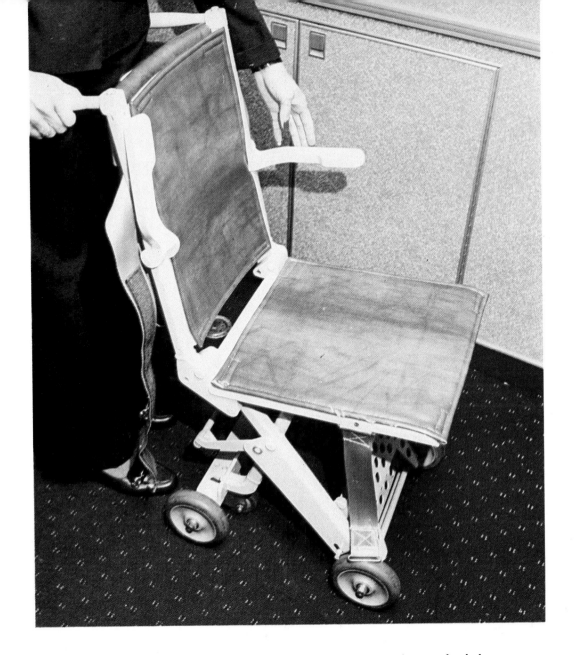

Next the stewardess shows the children a special chair. "This is a little wheelchair," she says. "It is used by passengers who can't walk and need to move about inside the airplane. It is small enough to go through the aisles."

The pilot and copilot are waiting to welcome the children, a few at a time, into the cockpit. They smile and chat, answering questions the children ask.

Leaving the airplane, the children pass
a restaurant and many shops. They all look
interesting. The children wish they could
stop, but they don't have time.

"People can find lots to do here while
they wait for their planes," says the guide.

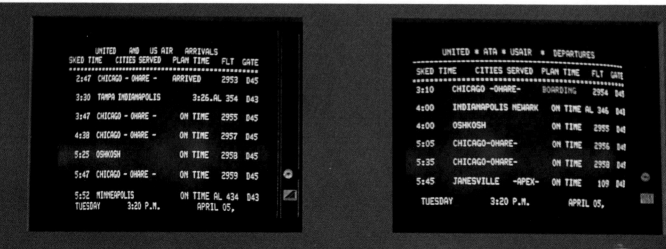

Sometimes, while people are waiting, they wonder if their planes will be on time. To find out, they look at computer monitors. Mr. Casper shows the children how to read the monitors.

Soon the children come to another terminal. What a big, busy place it is! The ticket counters look different here, but passengers still line up to buy tickets and check bags.

As they walk along, Mr. Casper says, "Look up high at the signs. They tell travelers things they need to know about the airport. Even people who don't speak English can find things by reading the pictures."

"Look," says Jill. "See the moving walkway. Will we go on it next?"

"Yes," Mrs. Dolan answers. And they
do.

When they get off the walkway, they see
windows up ahead. Looking out, they
watch workers putting fuel into a plane,
getting it ready to take off.

Another plane lands. Quickly workers begin unloading it. "What's in the big, gray box?" David asks.

"Empty lunch trays," says Mr. Casper. "And do you see the suitcase and car seat? They are going to baggage pickup. We will go there next."

At the baggage claim, everyone watches the suitcases riding by. Some people lift theirs off as they come by. Others let skycaps help them. But everyone checks to see that he has the right suitcase before he leaves.

Planes come and go all the time at such a busy airport. In the tower, men and women watch all the planes. They talk over radios with the pilots. They help the pilots land safely and take off again.

The children can see the tower from a window as they walk along.

Soon the children are back at the information desk where their visit began.

"I have something for you," says Mr. Casper. He pins wings on Peter.

The others hope they will get some too . . .

and they do — silver wings for everyone.

The children thank Mr. Casper. "You are
my favorite guide," says Tracy. "It's fun to
visit the airport."

"Yes, it is," says Mrs. Dolan. "But now it
is late . . . ."

So the children tell Mr. Casper good-
bye. They have to hurry to the bus. Their
driver will be waiting to take them back to
their school.

As they start home, some of the children look out of the bus window to see a plane taking off. "There it go-o-o-o-es," says Carlos.

How exciting! Everyone cheers.